Made in the USA
Coppell, TX
10 March 2023

14104901R00056